UN-FROG-GETTABLE RIDDLES

by Joanne E. Bernstein & Paul Cohen
pictures by Alexandra Wallner

Albert Whitman & Company, Chicago

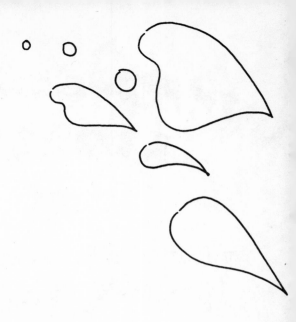

Library of Congress Cataloging in Publication Data

Bernstein, Joanne E.
    Un-frog-gettable riddles.

    Summary: A collection of frog riddles which provide
answers to questions such as "What side dish does
Frog usually enjoy?" and "What does Frog drink with
his favorite foods?"
    1. Riddles, Juvenile. 2. Frogs—Anecdotes,
facetiae, satire, etc. [1. Riddles. 2. Frogs—
Anecdotes, facetiae, satire, etc.] I. Cohen, Paul,
1945-. II. Wallner, Alexandra, ill. III. Title.
PN6371.5.B4   818'.5402   81-11548
ISBN 0-8075-8322-7   AACR2

For Andrew, who swamped us with riddles.
J.B.
For Marie, who can green and bear it.
P.C.

Fascinating Frog Facts

Which year is best for frogs?
What do you call a nervous frog?

Leap year.
A worry wart.

What's the difference between a bulldozer
    and a bullfrog?
What does a frog sit on?
What do you call a lying frog?
How does a frog put on pajamas?

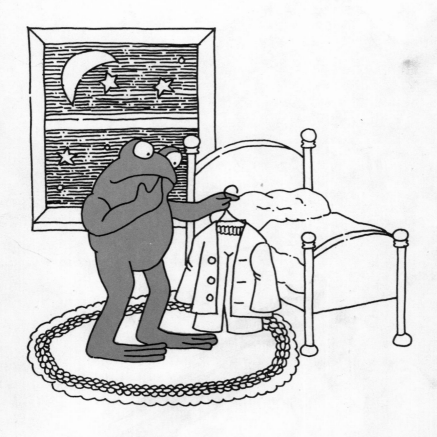

One sleeps, the other leaps.
A toadstool.
A fibbian.
One leg at a time.

Why are frogs like creatures from outer space?
How do frogs call to each other in the mist?
Why do frogs croak?
How can you tell where frogs are giving birth?

They're green Marsh-ans.
They use a froghorn.
They don't know the words.
Eggs mark the spot.

Frog Families Are Fun

What does Frog call his mother's sister?
How does Frog Junior remember his homework
    assignments?
How does Daddy Frog bring home flies from
    a restaurant?

Aunt-Phibian.
He writes them on his lily pad.
In a froggy bag.

What's Frog's favorite holiday?
Why is Mama Frog's hiding place like a book?
Why are baby tadpoles the best storytellers?
Which two flowers does Grandma Frog like best?
What did Mama Frog warn Baby Frog at the beach?

Mudder's Day.
It's a good reed.
Older frogs have lost their tales.
Croakuses and Frog-et-me-nots.
Watch out for the undertoad.

Some Frog History

What did Moses say to Pharaoh after the
　　plague?
Why did frogs cross the Atlantic Ocean on
　　Columbus's ship?
Where did most early frog pioneers settle?
Who came over on the Mayflower?

I toad you so.
It was too far to jump.
Greenland.
Our forefroggers.

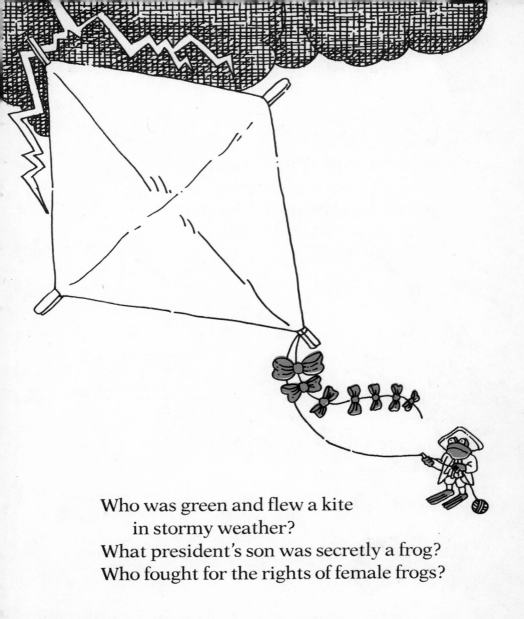

Who was green and flew a kite
　　in stormy weather?
What president's son was secretly a frog?
Who fought for the rights of female frogs?

Ben Froglin.
Tad Lincoln.
Susan B. Antoady.

Frogs of the Old Frontier

Where were the frontier tadpoles born?
Who was king of the green frontier?
Who is Frog's favorite frontier cowboy?
Who ran the Wild West Show?

In frog cabins.
Davy Croakit.
Hopalong Cassidy.
Buffalo Bill Toady.

Who was the greatest woman sharpshooter
  and sang "You Cain't Get a Frog with a Gun"?
What did Sitting Bull Frog use for money?
What did the Indians use to catch frogs?
What did Frog name his ranch?

Annie Croakley.
Swampum.
A toadempole.
The Pond-erosa.

More Famous Frogs

Who's green and gives out gifts at Christmas?
Who's green and gives out Easter eggs?
Who wrote the Frogs' cookbook?
Where does President Frog live?

Santa Frog.
Peter Ribbit.
Betty Croak-er.
In the Greenhouse, of course.

Name a frog composer.
How did Rocky Frog train for the big fight?
Which psychiatrist do all sad amphibians
    go to see?
Which famous tadpole was a nurse?
Who leaps twelve lily pads in a single bound?

Johann Sebastian Bog.
He used his jumprope.
Sigmund Frog.
Florence Nightingill. (Tadpoles have gills.)
Superfrog.

Frog Villains

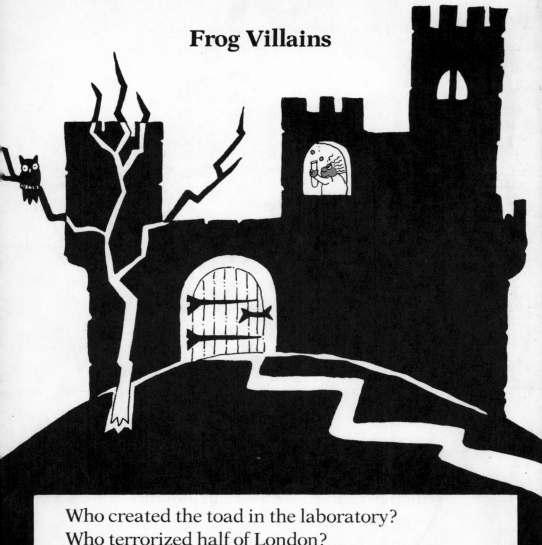

Who created the toad in the laboratory?
Who terrorized half of London?
Who was a dangerous frog outlaw of the Old West?

Dr. Frogenstein.
Jack the Flipper.
Billy the Tad.

What happened when the famous Frog Fly-Thief
	left his lily pad double-parked?
What did the police say when they arrested
	the famous Frog Fly-Thief?

It got toad away.
Aha—caught you green-handed.

Frogs Like to Eat

What does Frog order at the hamburger stand?
What does Frog order at the other hamburger
  stand?
What side dish does Frog usually enjoy?

Two all-fly patties, special sauce...
A hopper.
French flies.

What does Frog drink with his favorite foods?
What does Frog have for breakfast?
What would Frog order for a light snack?
How do frogs cook dinner?
Why are frogs thought to have bad table
 manners?

Croak-er cola.
Toadal.
Tea and croakers.
In a flying pan.
They're always sticking their tongues out.

Frog: Waiter, there's a fly in my soup.
Waiter: Only one? I'm sorry, I'll get you some more.

Frogs Are Good Sports

What kind of sportswear do frogs prefer?
What's the big event in the Frog Olympics?
Name a frog football team.

Jumpsuits.
Tadpole vaulting.
The Green Bay Packers.

What game do frogs play on the lawn?
What's another favorite lawn game?
Why do frogs swim?
What card game do fish play?

Croak-quet.
Leap Frog.
So they won't drown.
Go Frog.

When do frog baseball games start?
How does a frog catch a baseball?
What's a frog's favorite baseball game?
Who hit 714 flies out of the pond?

At the bug-inning.
In the webbing.
Catch-a-fly-is-up.
Babe Frog.

Frogs Work for a Living

Why are frogs great gardeners?
Where do frog doctors keep their patients?
How do frogs invest their money?
What is the frog baker's specialty?

They have green thumbs.
In the wading room.
In stocks and ponds.
Mud pie.

Why aren't there frogs in the army?
What do you call a frog dentist?
Why are frogs never without money?
Why do frogs make excellent plumbers?

They all have flat feet.
Unemployed—frogs don't have teeth.
They always have greenbacks.
They're good plungers.

Frog Entertainment

Do frogs stay up to watch TV?
What's Frog's favorite TV show?
Name a famous old song about a frog
    and a rabbit.
What was the greatest frog movie of all?
Who stars in the frog movies?

Yes, they enjoy the Lake, Lake Show.
Hoppy Days.
I Dream of Greenie with the Light Brown Hare.
Frog Wars.
Great stars include Mel Brooks, Jane Pond-a, Marsh-a Mason,
    and Amphibia Newton-John.

Frog Fairy Tales

What happened when the beautiful princess
    kissed the enchanted frog?
Who was green and slept for twenty years?
Who was green and slept for one hundred years?
How do frog fairy tales begin?

She got warts on her lips.
Ribbit Van Winkle.
Leaping Beauty.
Once upond a time …

And Some More Croaks...

Name three famous poles.
What do turtles wear in winter?
What do you call a frog who makes wise remarks?
Why did the frog cross the road?

North, South, and Tad.
Frogneck sweaters.
A wisecroaker.
He was glued to the chicken.

What do you call a frog from Libya?
How do little frogs grow?
What do you get when you cross a parrot
    with a frog?
What do you get when you cross a frog
    with a dinosaur?

A Libyan Amphibian.
By leaps and bounds.
A pollywog.
A giant leapin' lizard.

What do you call a park with a thousand
 frogs in it?
Why do frogs wear green suspenders?
Where do you get the best buys in frogs?
What's white outside, green inside, and hops?
What's brown outside, green inside, and hops?

A plague ground.
For camouflage.
At the bog-in basement.
A frog sandwich.
Frog on whole wheat.

What do you call a survey done by little frogs?
How do you get frogs off the trunk of your car?
What day comes after Thursday?

A tad-poll.
With a rear defrogger.
Frogday, what did you think?

PAUL COHEN is a science teacher whose lessons are often riddled with puns. When JOANNE BERNSTEIN, a college teacher of education, suggested they work together on her son's idea for a riddle book about frogs, Paul leaped at the opportunity.

ALEXANDRA WALLNER lives in an old farmhouse under a large apple tree in Woodstock, New York, with her husband, dog, and four cats. She enjoys working in her garden, cultivating wildflowers, and watching the changes each season brings to the country. Alexandra has recently developed more respect for the frogs and toads she finds lurking among the mossy rocks in the woods behind her house.